THE SCRIPTURE OF THE GOLDEN ETERNITY

Jack Kerouac

WITH INTRODUCTIONS BY
Anne Waldman and Eric Mottram

CITY LIGHTS San Francisco

THE SCRIPTURE OF THE GOLDEN ETERNITY
© 1960, 1970, 1994 by Jan Kerouac and Anthony Sampatakakos
All Rights Reserved
10 9 8 7 6 5 4 3
Originally published by Corinth Books, New York, 1960
Introduction © 1970 by Eric Mottram
Introduction © 1994 by Anne Waldman

Cover design by Rex Ray
Book design by Amy Scholder
Typesetting by Harvest Graphics

Library of Congress Cataloging-in-Publication Data
Kerouac, Jack, 1922-1969.
          Scripture of the golden eternity / by Jack Kerouac : with an
introduction by Eric Mottram.
          p.   cm. — (Pocket poets series)
          ISBN 0-87286-291-7 :
          1. Religious poetry, American. 2. Prose poems, American.
I. Title.
PS3521.E735S3   1994
811'.54—dc20
                                        94-2796
                                        CIP

City Lights Books are available to bookstores through our primary
distributor: Subterranean Company, P.O. Box 160, 265 S. 5th St.,
Monroe, OR 97456. 541-847-5274 Toll-free orders 800-274-7826. FAX
541-847-6018. Our books are also available through library jobbers and
regional distributors. For personal orders and catalogs, please write to
City Lights Books, 261 Columbus Avenue, San Francisco, CA 94133.

CITY LIGHTS BOOKS are edited by Lawrence Ferlinghetti and
Nancy J. Peters and published at the City Lights Bookstore,
261 Columbus Avenue, San Francisco, CA 94133.

Jack Kerouac died suddenly in 1969 at the age of 47.

INTRODUCTION TO THE
CITY LIGHTS EDITION

According to Jack Kerouac, Gary Snyder said to him at one point in the midst of their energetic comradeship, certainly sensing Jack's grasp of dharmic matters, "All right Kerouac, it's about time for you to write sutra." And Kerouac proceeded to pen his *Scripture of the Golden Eternity*. This was in 1956. Traditionally "sutra" comes from the Sanskrit root "siv," meaning to sew a thread or yarn. It also carries the implication of meeting point or junction, referring to the interstice of

Buddha's enlightenment with the student's understanding. A sutra is historically a dialogue between the Gotama & one or more of his disciples, and carries the orally delivered, exact words of the Buddha. Scripture, on the other hand, suggests the Christian canon — the Holy Scriptures or sacred writings of the Bible. Kerouac had a recondite knowledge, and appreciation, of both canons. And he's able in this remarkable text to get the two together in his own head, also throwing in a bit of Native American shamanism in the figure of Coyote. The form of this text is decidedly more Buddhist than Christian. It also teems with Kerouac's meticulous wit, his quirky sagacity.

Because the thinking's heady enough to make you crazy, there's a tendency in Buddhist matters to generate a magical language. To the outsider these illogical syllogisms sound like gibberish, double-speak. They're golden to a poet's ear. Sanskrit poetics speaks of *Sandhyabasha* or twilight speech, which is an "upside-down" language harboring contradictions and paradoxes. The Buddhist sutras, of which Kerouac's *Scripture* is so redolent, are filled with these contraries. Zen koans challenge the adept's brain, too, working not unlike Keats' notion of "negative capability" in which the mind may hold disparate views without any "irritable reaching after fact and reason." "The universe is fully known because it is / ignored." "Mother Kali eats herself back," or "Roaring dreams take place in a perfectly silent mind." "What does it mean that those trees and mountains are magic and unreal? It means that those trees and mountains are magic and unreal. What does it mean that those trees and mountains are not magic but real? It means those trees and mountains are not magic but real." "Opposites are not the same / for the same reason they are the same." Amen. Keroauc came to this topsy-turvy logic quite naturally.

The eminent Mahayana Buddhist literature entitled *The Prajnaparamita Sutra* or Perfection of Wisdom declares the quintessential teaching on the nature of form & emptiness, and Kerouac riffs on this conundrum quite a bit. Prajanaparamita, also called The Mother of the Buddhas, is the clear-witted awareness that the whole of reality is without origination or first cause. This wisdom sees through any reified notion of existence as well as through any nihilistic interpretation of life. We're all just conglomerations of tendencies, hopeless bundles of quivering meat bound on a wheel. We have no souls, no tangible selves. "thou'rt a numberless mass of sun-motes" says Jack's sutra. He's got an edge on impermanence: "the personalities / of long dead heroes are blank dirt." Or "The flies end up with the delicate viands." But this insight, rather than indulging cool cynicism, kindles tenderness. "Sociability is a big smile, and a big smile is / nothing but teeth. Rest and be kind." Or "Even in dreams be kind, because anyway there is no time, no space, no mind." Or "everything's alright, cats sleep." By digging on prajnaparamita even the duality between *samsara* (the wheel of suffering existence) and *nirvana* (release from suffering, i.e., bliss) is exceeded. Sparks of that perception give rise to generosity and *upaya* (skillful means). Kerouac's *Scripture* is accurately onto the profound dharma teaching of "form is emptiness, emptiness is form, Emptiness is no other than form, form is no other than emptiness" as in

> Both the word "God" and the essence of the word are emptiness, The form of emptiness which is emptiness having taken the form of form, is what you see and hear and feel right now, and what you taste and smell and think as you read this.

or

> Though it is everything, strictly speaking there is
> no golden eternity because everything is nothing:
> there are no things and no goings and comings: for
> all is emptiness, and emptiness is these forms,
> emptiness is this one formhood.

Co-emergent wisdom is the dharmic eidolon. This exists because, or doesn't. That doesn't exist because that doesn't exist either or because it also exists. Christian mysticism holds much of the same verbal subtlety. Kerouac quotes St. Therese's deceptively simple: "Love is all in all." Vigorous writer he is, Kerouac loves to frolic with words & their sense. Words like ideas like thoughts don't exist. They're all spun out of mind. And where does that come from? It's unborn. "Human Godhood is entertaining no notions whatsoever."

Kerouac's "satori" or flash of enlightenment comes, as he tells it, from a fainting spell ("I had apparently fainted, or died, for about sixty seconds") in his back yard. The "golden" is the sun on his eyelids. The "eternity" is everything and nothing, the everlasting "So." There's a tradition in Tibetan shamanism of the "delog," the one who dies and comes back to life to tell the story, the primordial "hit." This traveler-to-the-Bardo seer returns with a new understanding of emptiness & form, thereby lifts the consciousness of the rest of the tribe.

The Scripture of the Golden Eternity is fueled by Kerouac's discerning meditation on the nature of impermanence & consciousness, subtle like the dharma it invokes. We're here to disappear, therefore let's be as vivid & generous as we can. The intelligence & compassion behind this text is still alive.

Brother Jack extemporizes out of his timeless hipster scriptorium into the Void!

Boddhisattva Kerouac's diamond utterance cuts the space of ignorant grasping!

Read this, reread it, meditate upon it o ye poets & seekers & rejoice.

Anne Waldman
Martin Luther King Day 1994
The Jack Kerouac School of Disembodied Poetics
Boulder, Colorado

INTRODUCTION

To achieve personal peace in active joy in this century perhaps more than any other has meant dropping out of the current power structure. Since the Second World War for many men this has meant finding a viable alternative to the dragging decay of Christian capitalist democracy and the delusions of extreme leftist reform associated with the Depression and the Thirties. In the Forties and Fifties this alternative consisted in forms of ideological refusal to be held captive by the history of the West. *The Scripture of the Golden*

Eternity is Jack Kerouac's statement of confidence in his oneness with the universe of energy and form, a confidence to which his whole being swelled. His was not the search for the ecstasy of the mystic or psychedelic or the Artaud-mad. He sought a recognition in philosophy of his early sense that his body participated in the universal forms of energy with a quality of exuberance—that "serious exuberance" which he so accurately called jazz. How could he, a man of overflowing boundaries, live in a world of boundaries held rigid with coercion from the State and its educational agents? He lived out strategies of survival for the changing self, at first trying simply to recapture the sad boyhood happiness recorded in *The Town and the City* with such moving eloquence. For eloquence empowered his body towards others and the Other in a verbal erotic gesture of passion which filled both him and other people in a single embrace. But Kerouac knew the responsibility of his eloquence, and it is curiously near that of Scott Fitzgerald, whom he once called "the Alamoan / Huckster Crockett Hero / Who burned his Wife Down." In a letter of December 1949, he reminds us of the forlorn faith at the end of *The Great Gatsby*:

the place where the darkness of the trees by the river, on a starry night, gives hint of that inscrutable *future* Americans are always longing and longing for. And when they find that future, not till then, they begin looking *back*, with sorrows, and an understanding of how man haunts the earth, pacing, prowling, circling in the shades, and the intelligence of the compass, pointing to nothing in sight save starry passion.[1]

The *Scripture* is part of Kerouac's necessary going back as he perceives what the future may dismayingly hold. It recognizes the need for stillness within mobility, and the image he uses is there, too, in Henry Miller for the same purpose:

A hummingbird can come into a house and a hawk will not: so rest and be assured.

---

1   from a letter to Charles G. Sampas, quoted with permission from Ann Charters, Editor of *A bibliography of Works by Jack Kerouac*, The Phoenix Book Shop, Inc., New York, 1967

While looking for the light, you may suddenly be devoured by the darkness and find the true light.[2]

But Kerouac could rarely simply await the still moment. He lived the traditional life of the underground, of those who live out the double promises of Demeter and Persephone: you shall have both ecstasy and despair, and you will be reborn. His works are confessions of an American follower of Kore: the *Scripture* was composed in the Spring of 1956. Ten years later he told Ann Charters:

> Gary Snyder said, "All right Kerouac, it's about time for you to write a sutra." That's a thread of discourse, a scripture. He knew I was a Bodhi Sattva and had lived twelve million years in twelve million directions. You see, they really believe that, those maniacs.

2   from *Scripture* # 22

I'm a Catholic all along. I was really kidding
Gary Snyder. Boy, they're so gullible.[3]

Yet this noisy apparent denial is immediately and characteristically countered:

In pencil, carefully revised and everything,
because it was a scripture. I had no right to
be spontaneous.[4]

The seeker after IT in *On the Road*, the laughing religious, the artist, the American dionysiac of the historical underground always poised himself between spontaneity and discipline, a lesson he learned from jazz and Thomas Wolfe. But there remained the traditional American transcendental call from the East. As he wrote in *Book of Dreams*:[5]

3   Ann Charters, *op. cit.*, p. 20

4   *Ibid.*

5   *Book of Dreams*, City Lights Books, San Francisco, 1960

It broke my heart when I woke up, to realize that I was going to make that trip *East!* (pathetic!) — by myself — alone in eternity — to which now I go, on white horse, not knowing what's going to happen, predestined or not.

His exuberance — "my child's soul in a grown up body" — had to find its non-repressive training. His journeys were the experience of a karma directed towards eternal return:

> There were voyages, to California, lying on the ground, to Mexico, walking among the whores to the desert, the peotl and the t, to San Francisco of the endless green night — all nothing — I was back in Lowell, Sunday morning, the birds singing.

He dreamed also of being a great brakeman, and added to the lore of American heroes. He dreamed of being the Stavrogin of the football field. He dreamed of going "down in the underground sand caves of India." He dreamed of "choking in life . . . the stuff of karma" as he moved with "the great hegira of mankind in America." But as he wrote in "Rimbaud":[6]

> & it all adds up
> to nothing, like
> Dostoevsky, Beethoven
> or Da Vinci —

Throughout *Mexico City Blues*,[7] published three years after the *Scripture* was written, the presence of what Kerouac had learned he needed from Buddhism enlivens and guides the poet's desire for active equilibrium: "He Who is Free From Arbitrary Conceptions of Being or Non-Being" is his ideal. The danger is "my clever brain" — "the reason why there are so many things / Is because the mind breaks it up." But the Whole is there; fragmentation is to be allayed by contemplating the Oneness which is Nothing: "All is alone,

---

6   from *Yugen* # 6, 1960, also issued as a broadside by City Lights Books, 1960

7   *Mexico City Blues*, Grove Press, 1959

you dont have to talk." The "convulsive writer of poems" is steadied by "A great Sitter Under Trees." The political conflicts of the Cold War are set in perspective: "America is a permissible dream, / Providing you remember ants / Have Americas. . . ."

Kerouac's sutra is a controlled praise for the overwhelming sense of release afforded by contemplation of the "Dharma Law" which says: "All things is made of the same thing which is nothing," "the same thing which is essence," "pure nature," "the silence you hear inside the emptiness," "the movie in your mind." To steady his "big structure of Confession" he needed a universal assurance in which he could participate and which was not the dualistic conflict structure of Christianity. In his later thirties the Dantean horror of endless restlessness steadied around the Diamond Sutra interpreted as: "your goal is your starting place." His writer's faith began with: "the essence is realizable in words / That fade as they approach . . . the soul continues / In the same blinding light." So his work is, for all its apparent mobility, buoyed up among three formants: the life of the senses, the life of silence, and the life of religious duty — or karma, silence, and dharma.

The writing emerges then as a fulfillment of Whitman's old age ideals at Camden: "I don't want beautiful results — I want results: honest results: expression, expression."

Some of the choruses of *Mexico City Blues* play games with the Buddhist paradoxes and terms to which Snyder had turned Kerouac's attention. But the core of need and gratitude is firm, and from the 225th to the 242nd and last choruses, Kerouac has really controlled his sense of "restless mental searching" and his sense of loss of wholeness, through a beautiful inventiveness and exuberance of improvisation. The three choruses for Charley Parker bear witness to that love of controlled spontaneity he discovered earlier through Lester Young. Kerouac knew that spontaneity of the disciplined body enabled an artist to say "All is Well" without being either a bouncy charlatan or a relaxed antiquarian of comparative religion.

Since the *Scripture* appeared in 1960, ways of living through a traditional sense of oneness with all energy and form have become a common basis for survival in a disastrous time for the intelligent young in America. It is part of the legacy of the Beat Generation, and part of a constant recall to the value of poetry. In the words of Gary Snyder's "Notes on Poetry as an Ecological Survival Technique": poetry can be "the skilled and inspired use of the voice and language to embody rare and powerful states of mind that are in immediate origin personal to the singer, but at deep levels common to all who listen."[8]

The *Scripture* is an extraordinarily controlled use of a language and a process of discourse which at a crucial point in his career Kerouac could use to secure himself within that ecstatic love which continually slipped from his grasp by the sheer contingency of day to day living. The framework is traditional but freshly received information concerning how to end conflict and dualism. The message of *Book of Dreams* is here too:

8   Gary Snyder, *Earth House Hold*, New Directions, 1969, p. 117

Roaring dreams take place in a perfectly silent mind. Now that we know this, throw the raft away.[9]

Kerouac's Catholic training left part of him in need of confirmation in a possibility that moral commandment was not the religious center of the universe: "There are no warnings whatever issuing from the golden eternity: do what you want." He also found — and again Snyder's presence is keenly felt — that the original American already knew what the modern American attempted to retrieve from Buddhism. Where the Buddhist knows that the trees and mountains "are not magic but real," so the first American tells his own myth of reality:

"That looks like a tree, let's call it a tree," said Coyote to Earthmaker at the beginning.[10]

9   *Scripture* # 28
10 from *Scripture* # 66

It takes a powerful ego to plunge without irretrievable damage into a scripture of selflessness contemplating "the joyful mysterious essence of Arrangement." In 1970, the *Scripture* is a statement of what we have come to know as necessity: a joyful modesty as the condition of living in the universe without a restless urge to conquest, moral dogmatism and hierarchy. The "life of non-interference" which Dean Moriarty proposes to Sal Paradise is a "Tao decision." The Word which the beats of *On the Road*[11] awaited did not come from the form they shaped:

> . . . across the night, eastward over the Plains, where somewhere an old man with white hair was probably walking toward us with the Word, and would arrive any minute and make us silent.

The Word of Silence in fact came from the East but not as an ancient guru. It came through the old invitation

---

11   *On the Road*, Viking Press, 1967

taken up from Confucius, Thoreau and Pound, "Make it New" through direct study of the Buddhist path. That field of power vibrated for Emerson and for Whitman and still invites the young in America. Kerouac spent his mature life in that field, although his dark night was yet to come at the time of the confidence of *The Scripture of the Golden Eternity*:

> When you've understood this scripture, throw it away. If you cant understand this scripture, throw it away. I insist on your freedom.[12]

Eric Mottram
London
Summer 1970

12 *Scripture* # 45

THE
SCRIPTURE
OF THE
GOLDEN
ETERNITY

1

Did I create that sky? Yes, for, if it was
anything other than a conception in my mind
I wouldnt have said "Sky" — That is why I am the
golden eternity. There are not two of us here,
reader and writer, but one, one golden eternity,
One-Which-It-Is, That-Which-Everything-Is.

2

The awakened Buddha to show the way, the
chosen Messiah to die in the degradation
of sentience, is the golden eternity. One that
is what is, the golden eternity, or God, or,
Tathagata — the *name*. The Named One.
The human God. Sentient Godhood.
Animate Divine. The Deified One.
The Verified One. The Free One.
The Liberator. The Still One.
The Settled One. The Established One.
Golden Eternity. All is Well.
The Empty One. The Ready One.

The Quitter. The Sitter.
The Justified One. The Happy One.

3

That sky, if it was anything other than an
illusion of my mortal mind I wouldnt have said
"that sky." Thus I made that sky, I am the
golden eternity. I am Mortal Golden Eternity.

4

I was awakened to show the way, chosen to
die in the degradation of life, because I am
Mortal Golden Eternity.

5

I am the golden eternity in mortal animate form.

6

Strictly speaking, there is no me, because all is
emptiness. I am empty, I am non-existent.
All is bliss.

7

This truth law has no more reality than the world.

8

You are the golden eternity because there is
no me and no you, only one golden eternity.

9

The Realizer. Entertain no imaginations whatever,
for the thing is a no-thing. Knowing this then
is Human Godhood.

10

This world is the movie of what everything is,
it is one movie, made of the same stuff
throughout, belonging to nobody, which is what
everything is.

11

If we were not all the golden eternity we
wouldnt be here. Because we are here we
cant help being pure. To tell man to be pure on
account of the punishing angel that punishes the
bad and the rewarding angel that rewards the good
would be like telling the water "Be Wet" — Never
the less, all things depend on supreme reality,
which is already established as the record of
Karma-earned fate.

12

God is not outside us but is just us, the
living and the dead, the never-lived and
never-died. That we should learn it only now, is
supreme reality, it was written a long time ago
in the archives of universal mind, it is already
done, there's no more to do.

13

This is the knowledge that sees the golden
eternity in all things, which is us, you,
me, and which is no longer us, you, me.

14

What name shall we give it which hath no
name, the common eternal matter of the mind?
If we were to call it essence, some might think it
meant perfume, or gold, or honey. It is not even
mind. It is not even discussable, groupable into
words; it is not even endless, in fact it is not

even mysterious or inscrutably inexplicable; it is
what is; it is that; it is this. We could easily
call the golden eternity "This." But "what's in
a name?" asked Shakespeare. The golden eternity
by another name would be as sweet. A Tathagata,
A God, a Buddha by another name, an Allah, a Sri
Krishna, a Coyote, a Brahma, a Mazda, a Messiah,
an Amida, an Aremedeia, a Maitreya, a Palalakonuh,
1 2 3 4 5 6 7 8 would be as sweet. The golden
eternity is X, the golden eternity is A, the
golden eternity is △, the golden eternity is ○,
the golden eternity is □, the golden eternity is
t-h-e g-o-l-d-e-n e-t-e-r-n-i-t-y. In the
beginning was the word; before the beginning, in
the beginningless infinite neverendingness, was
the essence. Both the word "God" and the essence
of the word, are emptiness. The form of emptiness
which is emptiness having taken the form of form,
is what you see and hear and feel right now, and
what you taste and smell and think as you read
this. Wait awhile, close your eyes, let your
breathing stop three seconds or so, listen to
the inside silence in the womb of the world, let

your hands and nerve-ends drop, re-recognize
the bliss you forgot, the emptiness and
essence and ecstasy of ever having been and
ever to be the golden eternity. This is
the lesson you forgot.

15

The lesson was taught long ago in the other
world systems that have naturally changed
into the empty and awake, and are here
now smiling in our smile and scowling in our
scowl. It is only like the golden eternity
pretending to be smiling and scowling to
itself; like a ripple on the smooth ocean of
knowing. The fate of humanity is to vanish
into the golden eternity, return pouring into
its hands which are not hands. The navel shall
receive, invert, and take back what'd issued
forth; the ring of flesh shall close; the personalities
of long dead heroes are blank dirt.

16

The point is we're waiting, not how comfortable
we are while waiting. Paleolithic man waited by
caves for the realization of why he was there,
and hunted; modern men wait in beautified
homes and try to forget death and birth. We're
waiting for the realization that this is the
golden eternity.

17

It came on time.

18

There is a blessedness surely to be believed,
and that is that everything abides in
eternal ecstasy, now and forever.

19

Mother Kali eats herself back. All things but
come to go. All these holy forms, unmanifest,
not even forms, truebodies of blank bright
ecstasy, abiding in a trance, "in emptiness and
silence" as it is pointed out in the Diamond-cutter,
asked to be only what they are: *Glad.*

20

The secret God-grin in the trees and in the teapot,
in ashes and fronds, fire and brick, flesh and
mental human hope. All things, far from yearning
to be re-united with God, had never left themselves
and here they are, Dharmakaya, the body of the
truth law, the universal Thisness.

"Beyond the reach of change and fear, beyond
all praise and blame," the Lankavatara Scripture
knows to say, is he who is what he is in time and in
time-less-ness, in ego and in ego-less-ness, in self
and in self-less-ness.

Stare deep into the world before you as if it were
the void: innumerable holy ghosts, buddhies,
and savior gods there hide, smiling. All the
atoms emitting light inside wavehood, there is
no personal separation of any of it. A hummingbird
can come into a house and a hawk will not: so rest
and be assured. While looking for the light, you
may suddenly be devoured by the darkness
and find the true light.

23

Things dont tire of going and coming.
The flies end up with the delicate viands.

24

The cause of the world's woe is birth,
the cure of the world's woe is a bent stick.

25

Though it is everything, strictly speaking
there is no golden eternity because everything
is nothing: there are no things and no goings and
comings: for all is emptiness, and emptiness is
these forms, emptiness is this one formhood.

26

All these selfnesses have already vanished.
Einstein measured that this present universe is an
expanding bubble, and you know what that means.

27

Discard such definite imaginations of phenomena
as your own self, thou human being, thou'rt a
numberless mass of sun-motes: each mote a shrine.
The same as to your shyness of other selves,
selfness as divided into infinite numbers of beings,
or selfness as identified as one self existing
eternally. Be obliging and noble, be generous
with your time and help and possessions, and be
kind, because the emptiness of this little place
of flesh you carry around and call your soul,
your entity, is the same emptiness in every direction
of space unmeasurably emptiness, the same, one,
and holy emptiness everywhere: why be selfly and
unfree, Man God, in your dream? Wake up, thou'rt
selfless and free. "Even and upright your mind
abides nowhere," states Hui Neng of China.
We're all in Heaven now.

28

Roaring dreams take place in a perfectly silent
mind. Now that we know this, throw the raft away.

29

Are you tightwad and are you mean, those are
the true sins, and sin is only a conception of ours,
due to long habit. Are you generous and are
you kind, those are the true virtues, and they're
only conceptions. The golden eternity rests beyond
sin and virtue, is attached to neither, is attached
to nothing, is unattached, because the golden
eternity is Alone. The mold has rills but it is one
mold. The field has curves but it is one field.
All things are different forms of the same thing.
I call it the golden eternity — what do you
call it, brother? For the blessing and merit
of virtue, and the punishment and bad fate
of sin, are alike just so many words.

30

Sociability is a big smile, and a big smile is
nothing but teeth. Rest and be kind.

31

There's no need to deny that evil thing called
GOOGOO, which doesnt exist, just as there's no
need to deny that evil thing called Sex and Rebirth,
which also doesnt exist, as it is only a form of
emptiness. The bead of semen comes from a long
line of awakened natures that were your parent,
a holy flow, a succession of saviors pouring from
the womb of the dark void and back into it,
fantastic magic imagination of the lightning, flash,
plays, dreams, not even plays, dreams.

32

"The womb of exuberant fertility," Ashvhaghosha
called it, radiating forms out of its womb of
exuberant emptiness. In emptiness there is no
Why, no knowledge of Why, no ignorance of Why,
no asking and no answering of Why, and no
significance attached to this

33

A disturbed and frightened man is like the
golden eternity experimentally pretending at
feeling the disturbed-and-frightened mood; a
calm and joyous man, is like the golden eternity
pretending at experimenting with that experience;
a man experiencing his Sentient Being, is like
the golden eternity pretending at trying that out
too; a man who has no thoughts, is like the golden
eternity pretending at being itself; because
the emptiness of everything has no beginning
and no end and at present it is infinite.

34

"Love is all in all," said Sainte Thérèse, choosing
Love for her vocation and pouring out her
happiness, from her garden by the gate, with
a gentle smile, pouring roses on the earth,
so that the beggar in the thunderbolt received
of the endless offering of her dark void.
Man goes a-beggaring into nothingness.
"Ignorance is the father, Habit-Energy is
the Mother." Opposites are not the same
for the same reason they are the same.

35

The words "atoms of dust" and "the great
universes" are only words. The idea that they
imply is only an idea. The belief that we live here
in this existence, divided into various beings,
passing food in and out of ourselves, and casting off
husks of bodies one after another with no cessation
and no definite or particular discrimination, is
only an idea. The seat of our Immortal Intelligence

can be seen in that beating light between the eyes
the Wisdom Eye of the ancients: we know what
we're doing: we're not disturbed: because
we're like the golden eternity pretending at
playing the magic cardgame and making believe
it's real, it's a big dream, a joyous ecstasy of
words and ideas and flesh, an ethereal flower
unfolding and folding back, a movie, an
exuberant bunch of lines bounding emptiness,
the womb of Avalokitesvara, a vast secret
silence, springtime in the Void, happy young
gods talking and drinking on a cloud. Our
32,000 chillicosms bear all the marks of
excellence. Blind milky light fills our night;
and the morning is a crystal.

36

Give a gift to your brother, but there's no gift
to compare with the giving of assurance that he
is the golden eternity. The true understanding of
this would bring tears to your eyes. The other
shore is right here, forgive and forget, protect
and reassure. Your tormentors will be purified.
Raise thy diamond hand. Have faith and wait.
The course of your days is a river rumbling over
your rocky back. You're sitting at the bottom of the
world with a head of iron. Religion is thy sad
heart. You're the golden eternity and it must be
done by you. And means one thing: Nothing-
Ever-Happened. This is the golden eternity.

When the Prince of Kalinga severed the
flesh from the limbs and body of Buddha, even
then Buddha was free from any such ideas as
his own self, other self, living beings
divided into many selves, or living beings
united and identified into one eternal self.
The golden eternity isnt "me." Before you
can know that you're dreaming you'll wake up,
Atman. Had the Buddha, the Awakened One,
cherished any of these imaginary judgments
of and about things, he would have fallen
into impatience and hatred in his suffering.
Instead, like Jesus on the Cross he saw the
light and died kind, loving all living things.

38

The world was spun out of a blade of grass:
the world was spun out of a mind. Heaven
was spun out of a blade of grass: heaven was spun
out of a mind. Neither will do you much good,
neither will do you much harm. The Oriental
imperturbed, is the golden eternity.

39

He is called a Yogi, he is called a Priest,
a Minister, a Brahmin, a Parson, a Chaplain,
a Rôshi, a Laoshih, a Master, a Patriarch, a Pope,
a Spiritual Commissar, a Counselor, an Adviser,
a Bodhisattva-Mahasattva, an Old Man, a Saint,
a Shaman, a Leader, who thinks nothing of
himself as separate from another self, not
higher nor lower, no stages and no definite
attainments, no mysterious stigmata or secret
holyhood, no wild dark knowledge and no
venerable authoritativeness, nay a giggling sage
sweeping out the kitchen with a broom. After

supper, a silent smoke. Because there is no
definite teaching: the world is undisciplined
Nature endlessly in every direction inward
to your body and outward into space.

40

Meditate outdoors. The dark trees at night
are not really the dark trees at night, it's
only the golden eternity.

41

A mosquito as big as Mount Everest is much
bigger than you think; a horse's hoof is more
delicate than it looks. An altar consecrated to
the golden eternity, filled with roses and lotuses
and diamonds, is the cell of the humble prisoner,
the cell so cold and dreary. Boethius kissed the
Robe of the Mother Truth in a Roman dungeon.

Do you think the emptiness of the sky will ever
crumble away? Every little child knows that
everybody will go to heaven. Knowing that
nothing ever happened is not really knowing
that nothing ever happened, it's the golden eternity.
In other words, nothing can compare with telling
your brother and your sister that what happened,
what is happening, and what will happen, never
really happened, is not really happening and never
will happen, it is only the golden eternity.
Nothing was ever born, nothing will ever die.
Indeed, it didnt even happen that you heard about
golden eternity through the accidental reading of
this scripture. The thing is easily false. There
are no warnings whatever issuing from the
golden eternity: do what you want.

43

Even in dreams be kind, because anyway there is
no time, no space, no mind. "It's all not-born,"
said Bankei of Japan, whose mother heard this
from her son and did what we call "died happy."
And even if she had died unhappy, dying unhappy
is not really dying unhappy, it's the golden eternity.
It's impossible to exist, it's impossible to be
persecuted, it's impossible to miss your reward.

44

Eight hundred and four thousand myriads of
Awakened Ones throughout numberless swirls
of epochs appeared to work hard to save a grain
of sand, and it was only the golden eternity.
And their combined reward will be no greater and
no lesser than what will be won by a piece of
dried turd. It's a reward beyond thought.

45

When you've understood this scripture, throw it
away. If you cant understand this scripture,
throw it away. I insist on your freedom.

46

O Everlasting Eternity, all things and all truth
laws are no-things, in three ways, which is the
same way: AS THINGS OF TIME they dont
exist and never came, because they're already gone
and there is no time. AS THINGS OF SPACE they
dont exist because there is no furthest atom than
can be found or weighed or grasped, it is emptiness
through and through, matter and empty space too.
AS THINGS OF MIND they dont exist, because
the mind that conceives and makes them out does
so by seeing, hearing, touching, smelling, tasting,
and mentally-noticing and without this mind they
would not be seen or heard or felt or smelled or
tasted or mentally-noticed, they are discriminated
from that which they're not necessarily by imaginary

judgments of the mind, they are actually dependent
on the mind that makes them out, by themselves
they are no-things, they are really mental, seen only
of the mind, they are really empty visions of the
mind, heaven is a vision, everything is a vision.
What does it mean that I am in this endless universe
thinking I'm a man sitting under the stars on the
terrace of earth, but actually empty and awake
throughout the emptiness and awakedness of
everything? It means that I am empty and
awake, knowing that I am empty and awake,
and that there's no difference between me and
anything else. It means that I have attained
to that which everything is.

47

The-Attainer-To-That-Which-Everything-Is,
the Sanskrit Tathagata, has no ideas whatever
but abides in essence identically with the essence
of all things, which is what it is, in emptiness and
silence. Imaginary meaning stretched to make
mountains and as far as the germ is concerned it
stretched even further to make molehills. A
million souls dropped through hell but nobody
saw them or counted them. A lot of large people
isnt really a lot of large people, it's only the
golden eternity. When St. Francis went to heaven
he did not add to heaven nor detract from earth.
Locate silence, possess space, spot me the ego.
"From the beginning," said the Sixth Patriarch
of the China School, "not a thing is."

He who loves all life with his pity and
intelligence isnt really hc who loves all life
with his pity and intelligence, it's only natural.
The universe is fully known because it is
ignored. Enlightenment comes when you dont
care. This is a good tree stump I'm sitting on.
You cant even grasp your own pain let alone
your eternal reward. I love you because you're
me. I love you because there's nothing else
to do. It's just the natural golden eternity.

What does it mean that those trees and
mountains are magic and unreal? — It means
that those trees and mountains are magic and
unreal. What does it mean that those trees and
mountains are not magic but real? — it means
that those trees and mountains are not magic
but real. Men are just making imaginary
judgments both ways, and all the time it's
just the same natural golden eternity.

50

If the golden eternity was anything other than
mere words, you could not have said "golden
eternity." This means that the words are used
to point at the endless nothingness of reality.
If the endless nothingness of reality was anything
other than mere words, you could not have said
"endless nothingness of reality," you could not
have said it. This means that the golden eternity
is out of our word-reach, it refuses steadfastly
to be described, it runs away from us and leads
us in. The name is not really the name. The same
way, you could not have said "this world" if this
world was anything other than mere words. There's
nothing there but just that. They've long known
that there's nothing to life but just the living of it.
It Is What It Is and That's All It Is.

There's no system of teaching and no reward
for teaching the golden eternity, because
nothing has happened. In the golden eternity
teaching and reward havent even vanished let alone
appeared. The golden eternity doesnt even have to
be perfect. It is very silly of me to talk about
it. I talk about it because there's no command or
warning of any kind, and also no blessing and no
reward. I talk about it simply because here I am
dreaming that I talk about it in a dream already
ended, ages ago, from which I'm already awake, and
it was only an empty dreaming, in fact nothing
whatever, in fact nothing ever happened at all.
The beauty of attaining the golden eternity is
that nothing will be acquired, at last.

Kindness and sympathy, understanding and
encouragement, these give: they are better
than just presents and gifts: no reason in the
world why not. Anyhow, be nice. Remember
the golden eternity is yourself. "If someone will
simply practice kindness," said Gotama to
Subhuti, "he will soon attain highest perfect
wisdom." Then he added: "Kindness after all
is only a word and it should be done on the spot
without thought of kindness." By practicing
kindness all over with everyone you will soon
come into the holy trance, definite distinctions
of personalities will become what they really
mysteriously are, our common and eternal blissstuff,
the pureness of everything forever, the great bright
essence of mind, even and one thing everywhere the
holy eternal milky love, the white light everywhere
everything, emptybliss, svaha, shining, ready, and
awake, the compassion in the sound of silence, the
swarming myriad trillionaire you are.

53

Everything's alright, form is emptiness and
emptiness is form, and we're here forever, in
one form or another, which is empty. Everything's
alright, we're not here, there, or anywhere.
Everything's alright, cats sleep.

54

The everlasting and tranquil essence, look around
and see the smiling essence everywhere. How
wily was the world made, Maya, not-even-made.

55

There's the world in the daylight. If it was
completely dark you wouldnt see it but it would
still be there. If you close your eyes you really see
what it's like: mysterious particle-swarming
emptiness. On the moon big mosquitos of straw
know this in the kindness of their hearts. Truly
speaking, unrecognizably sweet it all is.
Dont worry about nothing.

56

Imaginary judgments about things, in this
Nothing-Ever-Happened wonderful Void,
you dont even have to reject them, let alone
accept them. "That looks like a tree, let's
call it a tree," said Coyote to Earthmaker at
the beginning, and they walked around the
rootdrinker patting their bellies.

57

Perfectly selfless, the beauty of it, the butterfly
doesnt take it as a personal achievement, he just
disappears through the trees. You too, kind and
humble and not-even-here, it wasnt in a greedy
mood that you saw the light that belongs to
everybody.

58

Look at your little finger, the emptiness of it is
no different than the emptiness of infinity.

59

Cats yawn because they realize
that there's nothing to do.

60

Up in heaven you wont remember all these
tricks of yours. You wont even sigh "Why?"
Whether as atomic dust or as great cities, what's
the difference in all this stuff. A tree is still
only a rootdrinker. The puma's twisted face
continues to look at the blue sky with sightless
eyes, Ah sweet divine and indescribable verdurous
paradise planted in mid-air! Caitanya, it's only
consciousness. Not with thoughts of your mind,
but in the believing sweetness of your heart,
you snap the link and open the golden door
and disappear into the bright room, the everlasting
ecstasy, eternal Now. Soldier, follow me! — there
never was a war. Arjuna, dont fight! — why
fight over nothing? Bless and sit down.

61

I remember that I'm supposed to be a man and
consciousness and I focus my eyes and the
print reappears and the words of the poor book
are saying, "The world, as God has made it"
and there are no words in my pitying heart
to express the knowless loveliness of the
trance there was before I read those words,
I had no such idea there was a world.

62

This world has no marks, signs or evidence of
existence, nor the noises in it, like accident
of wind or voices or heehawing animals,
yet listen closely the eternal hush of silence
goes on and on throughout all this, and has been
going on, and will go on and on. This is because
the world is nothing but a dream and is just thought
of and the everlasting eternity pays no attention
to it. At night under the moon, or in a quiet
room, hush now, the secret music of the Unborn

goes on and on, beyond conception, awake beyond existence. Properly speaking, awake is not really awake because the golden eternity never went to sleep: you can tell by the constant sound of Silence which cuts through this world like a magic diamond through the trick of your not realizing that your mind caused the world.

63

The God of the American Plateau Indian was Coyote. He says: "Earth! those beings living on your surface, none of them disappearing, will all be transformed. When I have spoken to them, when they have spoken to me, from that moment on, their words and their bodies which they usually use to move about with, will all change. I will not have heard them."

64

I was smelling flowers in the yard, and when
I stood up I took a deep breath and the blood all
rushed to my brain and I woke up dead on my
back in the grass. I had apparently fainted,
or died, for about sixty seconds. My neighbor
saw me but he thought I had just suddenly
thrown myself on the grass to enjoy the sun.
During that timeless moment of unconsciousness
I saw the golden eternity. I saw heaven. In it
nothing had ever happened, the events of a
million years ago were just as phantom and
ungraspable as the events of now or of a million
years from now, or the events of the next ten
minutes. It was perfect, the golden solitude, the
golden emptiness, Something-Or-Other, something
surely humble. There was a rapturous ring of
silence abiding perfectly. There was no question
of being alive or not being alive, of likes and
dislikes, of near or far, no question of giving
or gratitude, no question of mercy or judgment,
or of suffering or its opposite or anything.

It was the womb itself, aloneness, alaya vijnana
the universal store, the Great Free Treasure, the
Great Victory, infinite completion, the joyful
mysterious essence of Arrangement. It seemed
like one smiling smile, one adorable adoration,
one gracious and adorable charity, everlasting
safety, refreshing afternoon, roses, infinite
brilliant immaterial golden ash, the Golden Age.
The "golden" came from the sun in my eyelids,
and the "eternity" from my sudden instant
realization as I woke up that I had just
been where it all came from and where it
was all returning, the everlasting So, and
so never coming or going; therefore I call it
the golden eternity but you can call it anything
you want. As I regained consciousness I felt so sorry
I had a body and a mind suddenly realizing I
didnt even have a body and a mind and nothing
had ever happened and everything is alright
forever and forever and forever, O thank you
thank you thank you.

65

This is the first teaching from
the golden eternity.

66

The second teaching from the golden eternity
is that there never was a first teaching
from the golden eternity. So be sure.

CITY LIGHTS PUBLICATIONS

Higman, Perry, tr. LOVE POEMS FROM SPAIN AND SPANISH
    AMERICA
Jaffe, Harold. EROS: ANTI-EROS
Jenkins, Edith. AGAINST A FIELD SINISTER
Katzenberger, Elaine, ed. FIRST WORLD, HA HA HA!: The
    Zapatista Challenge
Kerouac, Jack. BOOK OF DREAMS
Kerouac, Jack. POMES ALL SIZES
Kerouac, Jack. SCATTERED POEMS
Kerouac, Jack. SCRIPTURE OF THE GOLDEN ETERNITY
Lacarrière, Jacques. THE GNOSTICS
La Duke, Betty. COMPAÑERAS
La Loca. ADVENTURES ON THE ISLE OF ADOLESCENCE
Lamantia, Philip. BED OF SPHINXES: SELECTED POEMS
Lamantia, Philip. MEADOWLARK WEST
Laughlin, James. SELECTED POEMS: 1935–1985
Laure. THE COLLECTED WRITINGS
Le Brun, Annie. SADE: On the Brink of the Abyss
Mackey, Nathaniel. SCHOOL OF UDHRA
Masereel, Frans. PASSIONATE JOURNEY
Mayakovsky, Vladimir. LISTEN! EARLY POEMS
Morgan, William. BEAT GENERATION IN NEW YORK
Mrabet, Mohammed. THE BOY WHO SET THE FIRE
Mrabet, Mohammed. THE LEMON
Mrabet, Mohammed. LOVE WITH A FEW HAIRS
Mrabet, Mohammed. M'HASHISH
Murguía, A. & B. Paschke, eds. VOLCAN: Poems from Central
    America
Murillo, Rosario. ANGEL IN THE DELUGE
Nadir, Shams. THE ASTROLABE OF THE SEA
Parenti, Michael. AGAINST EMPIRE
Parenti, Michael. BLACKSHIRTS & REDS
Parenti, Michael. DIRTY TRUTHS
Pasolini, Pier Paolo. ROMAN POEMS
Pessoa, Fernando. ALWAYS ASTONISHED
Peters, Nancy J., ed. WAR AFTER WAR (City Lights Review #5)
Poe, Edgar Allan. THE UNKNOWN POE
Porta, Antonio. KISSES FROM ANOTHER DREAM
Prévert, Jacques. PAROLES
Purdy, James. THE CANDLES OF YOUR EYES
Purdy, James. GARMENTS THE LIVING WEAR